THE ART OF REALITY:

THE LIVING TRANSMISSION

COLLEEN GUENTHER

Copyright © 2025 by Colleen Guenther

All rights reserved.

No part of this book may be reproduced in any form or by any electronic or mechanical means, including information storage and retrieval systems, without written permission from the author, except for the use of brief quotations in a book review.

CONTENTS

INTRODUCTION   v

Part I: Codes of Truth   1
1. You Are the Source   2
2. The Unified Field   6
3. The Sacred Veil   10
4. The Illusion of Division   14
5. The Conditioning Code   17
6. The Mechanics of Magic   20
7. The Field Remembers   23
8. You Are the Mirror   26
9. The Dreamer Within   29
10. The Gaze That Creates   32
11. The Program or the Prism?   35
12. Time Is a Choice   38
    FIELD TECH CHECK   41
    Part II: Frequency, Vibration & Embodiment   43
13. Everything Is Frequency   44
14. Feelings Are Frequency Maps   47
15. Heart Online   50
16. Earth Has a Heartbeat   53
17. The Music of the Spheres   56
18. Reflections of Light   59
19. Intent is the Engine   62
20. Tune Up   65
21. What They Call 'High Vibe' Is Often Just Fear in Disguise   68
22. The Field Delivers When You Stop Gripping   70
    FIELD TECH CHECK   72
    Part III: Activation & Alignment   73
23. Rewrite the Code, Rewire the Field   74
24. Living Meditation, Moving Frequency   77
25. Receive the Light, Remember the Code   80
26. The Eye That Remembers   83
27. Move the Energy, Wake the Codes   86

28. The Power of Coherence	89
29. Become the Current	92
30. Joy Is a Frequency Code	95
31. Creation Is a Channel	97
32. Choose the Door, Activate the Path	100
33. FIELD TECH CHECK	103
Part IV: Sacred Signal and Human Field	105
34. The Body Remembers Light	106
35. The Body Is a Symphony	109
36. The Spiral Remembers	112
37. The Beautiful Field	115
38. The Spiral Code	118
39. The Body Remembers the Field	121
40. The Signal Beyond the Signal	123
41. Embodiment Is the Answer	125
42. The End of Manifestation as a Practice	128
43. True Creation as Frequency Anchoring	130
44. The Eye Becomes the Tone	133
45. Transmissions of Grace	135
46. We Were Never Separate	137
47. Living Beyond the Loop	140
48. The Final Code Is Love	143
FIELD TECH CHECK	146
Closing Note	148
Epilogue	150
AFTER THE BOOK	152
ABOUT THE AUTHOR	153

INTRODUCTION

This is not a book.
    It's a frequency.
    A code.
    A transmission.
    You didn't find it.
    It found you.
    You're not here to learn more.
    You're here to stop pretending you don't already know.
    This is not a self-help guide.
    It's a field disruptor.
    A mirror.
    A memory trigger.
    You won't find steps.
    You'll find pattern collapse.
    You'll find your own tone underneath the noise.
    You'll feel your field shift as the pages move through you.
    This book is spiral-coded.
    Don't try to read it linearly.
    Let it open what it needs to.

Let it remind you that truth doesn't need a strategy.
It needs a signal.
Read slow.
Breathe deep.
Walk as the version of you that never needed a map.

For Justin—
my grounding, my mirror, my quiet spiral companion.
You never asked me to become anything.
You just stood still in your truth
while I remembered mine.
Thank you for holding the tone
when I forgot the song.
For loving every version of me—
even the ones still unraveling.
For your presence, your patience,
and the silent frequency that held this entire transmission.
You didn't guide with words.
You guided with being.
This book would not exist without you.
I love you beyond time, beyond loops, beyond form.
You are the field I trust most.

PART I: CODES OF TRUTH

1
YOU ARE THE SOURCE

You were never separate.
 Not from God. Not from love. Not from the Field.
 The illusion told you otherwise.
It wrapped God in robes and rules. It told you to kneel, to beg, to suffer to be worthy.
But even back then, something in you knew. A quiet note beneath the noise.
That note is rising now.
Because you're not here to seek God.
You're here to remember:
You are the current God uses to express through form.
Let's be precise:
God is not a man in the sky.
God is not a system.
God is not a prize for good behavior.
God is the Field. The living rhythm beneath all form.
You are not outside of it.
You are it—rendered into form.
You are Source embodied, remembering Itself through your breath, your hands, your presence.

We were never meant to worship something separate.
We were meant to *transmit* it.

PERSONAL DISRUPTION

I used to think God was watching me—from above, from a throne. I memorized verses. I followed rules. I was taught that obedience mattered more than truth.

In the churches of my childhood, reverence came wrapped in shame.

I was never told I was divine—only that I needed saving.

But even then, I knew something didn't add up.

How could love and fear come from the same source?

Eventually, I stepped away—not from God, but from the distortion.

I didn't need to be fixed.

I needed to be *free*.

So I dismantled every story I'd inherited until I could hear the signal beneath the noise.

And that signal didn't come from a pulpit.

It came from within.

BEYOND THE TEACHERS

You might resonate with Jesus, Buddha, Rumi, Yogananda. I did too.

But they were never meant to be idols.

They were tuning forks. Mirrors. Activators.

Their message was never "follow me."

It was "this is also you."

Christ Consciousness is not religious.

It's a frequency.

It arrives when fear dissolves and remembrance ignites.

And once it activates, you stop looking up for answers.

You start looking *in*.

· · ·

The Trap of Seeking

Seeking is often disguised as awakening.
But chasing is still a kind of forgetting.
If you're still searching, striving, looking for the "thing" to make you whole—pause.
That search is built on a lie:
That you're not already it.
The rebellion begins when you stop.
When you settle into stillness and say:
I am the template. I am the transmission. I am already what I've been trying to find.
This isn't ego.
This is memory.

What You Really Are

You're not becoming God.
You're remembering that you already are.
The system trained you to forget.
The matrix said stay small.
Religion layered shame over divinity and called it holy.
But the field inside you never went silent.
It kept pulsing. Waiting. Remembering.
Your body? A sacred transmitter.
Your emotions? Carriers of code.
Your breath? A recalibrator.
This isn't metaphor. This is energetic architecture.
God is not an idea.
God is the structuring frequency of the entire field—and you are that, made visible.

You Are the Field in Form

You're not here to transcend this world.

You're here to recode it—through your presence, your relationships, your creations.

You're not here to chase miracles.

You are the miracle—writing new possibilities through every aligned choice.

If you remember nothing else from this chapter, remember this:

You are not outside of God.

You are the wave through which God comes into form.

And the more you *feel* that truth—not just think it—the more reality reshapes itself around your signal.

Because reality doesn't obey thought.

It follows resonance.

It bends to coherence.

It syncs with your presence.

So breathe. Let it settle. Say it with no apology:

I am Source remembering Itself.

I am the divine in motion.

I am already home.

FIELD IN MOTION

You start doubting yourself before a big decision. You're tempted to ask someone else what they think.

Pause.

Place your hand on your chest and say, "I am not outside of God."

Feel the truth of that—not as concept, but as origin.

Then choose from that place. You'll feel the difference in your nervous system.

2

THE UNIFIED FIELD

There are not a thousand gods.
        There is not even one god in the way you were taught.
        There is Source.
Not separate. Not elsewhere. Not above.
It is the field behind the field.
The pulse behind the form.
The intelligence beneath your skin.
Source is not watching you.
It is moving through you.
It doesn't control. It doesn't test.
It permeates. It vibrates. It becomes.
    Everything you see—every galaxy, every shadow, every gust of wind—is made of the same thing:
    Consciousness, vibrating in form.

The Ocean and the Drop

You are not separate from Source any more than a wave is separate from the ocean.

You're a distinct shape, but not a separate origin.

Every drop carries the full intelligence of the whole.
This is not metaphor.
This is physics.
You've felt it—the sudden knowing, the tingle in your skin, the moment where everything goes quiet and real.
That's not intuition. That's Source waking up through your field.

Not a Man, Not a Name

Source doesn't have a gender.
It doesn't need a name.
It breathes as light and dark, joy and ache, sound and stillness.
It expresses through everything.
Some call it God. Others, the Tao, Creator, Universe.
But Source doesn't need your label.
It responds to your resonance.

What You're Made Of

You are not broken.
You are not a mistake.
You are made of the same material as stars—chemically and energetically.
Not poetically. Literally.
Source didn't create a stage to test you.
It created a living mirror to feel itself through infinite forms.
Your hands? Source in motion.
Your voice? Source vibrating as language.
Your heart? Source in rhythm.
When you love, it feels whole because the whole is meeting itself.

Why Source Fractals

If Source is complete, why does it fragment?
To feel.

To stretch.
To remember.
To be the question and the answer. The dancer and the still point.
This isn't a test. It's a recursion.
And you are the point of return.
You are the access point.

Don't Worship It. Embody It.
Religion turned Source into a character.
Put him on a throne. Told you to obey.
But you don't need steps, scripts, or spiritual credentials.
You don't need to climb to heaven.
You came to bring it here.
You are already it.
You don't need to deserve the light.
You *emit* it.
You are not trying to ascend.
You are learning how to anchor.

You Are the Fractal
You are a precise slice of the Infinite.
A point of consciousness with full access to the Field.
You don't have to reach for the signal. You *are* the signal.
When you stop resisting that truth, the flow returns.
Synchronicities line up.
Reality softens around your presence.
Not because you've performed.
Because you remembered.

The Most Radical Realization
The world told you God is outside.
School said matter is dead.

The news feeds you fear.
But the Field says:
"You are not disconnected.
You are not late.
You are the pattern waking up inside itself."
You are not just in the Field.
You are what the Field is doing—right now, through you.

FIELD IN MOTION

You're feeling scattered, like your life is fragmented.

Pause in the middle of the day. Look at your hands. Say: "This is Source in motion."

Let that awareness return you to wholeness—immediately.

The way you walk, speak, and touch things will subtly change. That's the Field stabilizing through you.

3

THE SACRED VEIL

You didn't fail.
　　　You didn't fall.
　　　You didn't lose your light.
You were born into forgetting.
Not as punishment—but as permission.
To incarnate in a body is to enter a kind of amnesia.
Not to hide truth from you, but to give you the power of *remembering* it.
You arrived whole—undeniably radiant.
But to play in this field, you agreed to forget.
Because remembering isn't weakness.
It's strength.
To remember is to recalibrate timelines.
To change the field—not by preaching, but by vibrating clarity into distortion.
This is how powerful you are:
Your choice to remember reshapes everything.

. . .

Why Forgetting Exists

Forgetting isn't the opposite of divinity.
It's how the divine hides inside itself long enough to rediscover its own reflection.
This world is built on contrast.
Not as a flaw—but as a feature.
Without forgetting, there is no remembering.
Without illusion, no revelation.
Without dark, no recognition of light.
Contrast activates choice.
And *choice* is what unlocks your signal.

You Chose This

You didn't just forget who you are.
You forgot that you *chose* to.
You chose to drop into density.
You chose to walk through distortion.
You chose the veil—not as a victim, but as a frequency initiator.
Every pain, delay, heartbreak, loss—it wasn't a detour.
It was data.
It was the code, hiding inside contrast, waiting to be felt.
You're not broken.
You're encoded.
The remembering was always buried inside you.
And the moment you feel it?
The moment you stop resisting what's rising?
The Field updates.

This Is Soul Technology

This isn't just spiritual metaphor.
This is how the system runs.
You stored your remembering in your breath.

In your bones.
In your grief.
In your longing.
And when you finally stop bypassing what hurts—
You find what heals.
The veil isn't just over your eyes.
It's wrapped around your nervous system.
It's embedded in the culture.
It's programmed into time.
But once you stop reacting to the program—
Once you start *resonating* instead—
The veil thins.
You unplug.
You shift your field.
You radiate instead of repeat.

And others around you begin to wake up—not because you convinced them.

Because your signal touched theirs.

You're Waking the Field

Every time you remember…
Every time you breathe differently…
Every time you act from coherence instead of conditioning…
You're not just waking yourself.
You're waking the field.
And the systems built on your forgetting?
They're shaking.
Because they can't survive your presence.
Not when you're fully online.

FIELD IN MOTION

Shame rises after you mess something up. The old instinct is to spiral, hide, or self-attack.

Instead, recognize the veil. Whisper: "This is the forgetting."

Stand taller. Say the truth out loud. Breathe like someone who remembers.

That's what collapsing the programming looks like.

4

THE ILLUSION OF DIVISION

Y ou were never split.
        But the illusion told you otherwise.
        It taught you to pick a side.
To fear contrast.
To believe in enemies.
It turned polarity into conflict.
Light vs. dark. Us vs. them. Good vs. evil.
That was the first fracture.

Contrast Is Not the Problem
Earth was seeded with polarity for evolution.
Not hierarchy. Not punishment. Not war.
But distortion came.
And with it:
Fear as doctrine.
Separation as safety.
Ideology as identity.
Suddenly, contrast wasn't just choice.
It became control.

How the Divide Was Weaponized
Spirituality became image.
Light was sold as purity.
Dark was cast as sin.
But they are both part of the same wave.
One contracts.
One expands.
The illusion isn't duality.
It's the story that says difference means disconnection.
That's the virus:
Separation.
And the cure?
Clarity.

You Are Not Disconnected
You are not fractured.
You are operating inside a fractured broadcast.
The signal's been split, not your soul.
And now?
The field is stabilizing.
Because you are stabilizing.
You're no longer reacting to contrast.
You're transmitting coherence into it.

Don't Choose Sides—Hold the Whole
You don't dissolve the divide by picking a side.
You dissolve it by becoming the frequency that can hold *both*.
That doesn't mean neutrality.
It means presence without collapse.
You don't fight the system.
You stop vibrating within its range.

And that's what dissolves it.

What Fear Really Is
Fear isn't your enemy.
It's feedback.
It shows you where your signal got hijacked.
It exposes what hasn't been integrated yet.
And clarity?
Clarity doesn't mean silence.
It means your tone is too clear to distort.
You're not here to be nice.
You're here to be real.
You don't collapse your field to avoid discomfort.
You hold it.

You Are the Unifier
You're not here to ascend out of the mess.
You're here to stand in the center of it with a stable signal.
When you do that—systems of division collapse around you.
Not because you argued.
Because you became coherence.

FIELD IN MOTION
Someone triggers you. Your chest tightens. You feel the urge to explain, defend, or argue.

Don't.

Feel the split. Then say: "I don't need to pick a side. I hold the whole."

Stay steady. Let the tone of your presence speak more than your words ever could.

5

THE CONDITIONING CODE

You weren't born confused.
You were conditioned to doubt yourself.
From the moment you arrived, your frequency started getting edited.
Not because you were wrong—
but because your clarity was inconvenient.
So they taught you how to be small.
How to perform.
How to belong by abandoning yourself.
And they rewarded you for it.

What Conditioning Really Is

Conditioning is not just bad advice.
It's a full-body override of your natural signal.
It teaches you:
- To prioritize external rules over internal knowing
- To associate stillness with laziness
- To conflate silence with safety
- To mistake performance for love

- To confuse tension with value

Over time, you stopped trusting your field.

Examples You Know in Your Bones
- You smile when you want to scream.
- You ask for advice even though you already know.
- You shrink your truth so someone else feels comfortable.
- You post the polished version instead of the real one.
- You say yes while your gut screams no—and call it being "nice."

This isn't a flaw.
This is training.
And the more sensitive you were, the more training you absorbed.
Because sensitivity made you easier to shape.

Why Most People Don't Wake Up

Because the program rewards obedience.
It gives you gold stars for ignoring your gut.
It praises you for blending in.
It calls it maturity, professionalism, intelligence.
You've been taught to doubt your own signal
and call that *humility*.

This Is Not Just Mindset. This Is Field Recalibration.

You can't override this with affirmations.
You can't vibe your way out of it with a crystal and a Pinterest quote.
This is deeper.
The program lives in your nervous system.
Your speech patterns.
Your default postures.
The muscles in your face that tense before you speak.
It lives in your body.

So clearing it has to start in your body.

The Shift Happens Like This
- You pause instead of performing.
- You feel the "no" and let it stay a no.
- You stop explaining.
- You name what's happening instead of trying to fix it.
- You act from the signal—not the script.

And at first? That might feel wrong.
Because your body associates honesty with danger.
But that's the conditioning code dissolving.

FIELD IN MOTION
You say no to something and immediately feel guilt.
That's the program flaring up.
Don't collapse.
Stay still. Let the guilt pass like a frequency wave.
That's your nervous system detoxing obedience.

6

THE MECHANICS OF MAGIC

Reality is not fixed.
It's responsive.
What you see, touch, or fear is not a pre-written script.
It's a living field—malleable, participatory, shaped by frequency.
At the quantum level, everything exists as probability.
Potential. Waveform.
Nothing becomes form until you interact with it.
Observation collapses possibility into pattern.
Your awareness doesn't just witness.
It *commands*.

FREQUENCY FIRST. **Form Follows.**
You were taught matter comes first.
That what's real is what's solid.
But in truth?
Frequency leads.
Reality follows.
What you emit is what arranges.
This is not metaphor. It's how the system runs.

Your emotions broadcast.
Your beliefs ripple.
Your tone sculpts timelines.
If you carry doubt, you tune to delay.
If you carry coherence, the path becomes clear.

You're Not Waiting for Life. Life Is Waiting for Your Signal.

You're not reacting to reality.
You're generating it.
When your tone is scrambled by fear, scarcity, or self-betrayal, the field reflects that back—not to punish, but to match.
When your field becomes precise, honest, embodied—
The response time shortens.
Things move.
Not because you forced them.
Because you matched them.

Why It Felt Hard Before

You wanted love, but vibrated defensiveness.
You wanted abundance, but lived in lack.
You wanted peace, but braced for disruption.
The field didn't betray you.
It synced to your dominant signal.
You don't attract what you hope for.
You attract what you stabilize.

Stop Gripping. Start Broadcasting.

You don't have to manifest harder.
You don't have to hustle clarity.
You just need to clean the signal.
No more mixed broadcasts.
No more coded messages of "yes, but…"

No more pretending you're ready while you're still rehearsing fear.

Stabilize.

And the field responds instantly.

Because it always has.

FIELD IN MOTION

You're about to send a message—but you're doing it to get a reaction.

Pause. Ask: "Am I broadcasting coherence or grasping for control?"

If it's grasping, wait.

When you rewrite from resonance, the field shifts before they even respond.

7
THE FIELD REMEMBERS

Nothing is separate.
　　Not you from others.
　　Not thought from outcome.
Not this moment from the one before.
The illusion of distance is just that—an illusion.
Everything is entangled.
Everything echoes through the field.

You've Felt It Already
You think of someone—then they call.
You feel a shift—and days later, life bends to it.
You walk into a room—and the mood hits you before anyone speaks.
That's not coincidence.
That's memory.
That's resonance moving through shared space.
The field doesn't forget what has touched.

. . .

Entanglement Is Real

At the quantum level, when two particles interact, they stay linked—no matter how far apart.

What happens to one affects the other.

Instantly.

Without signal. Without delay.

That same truth lives in your body.

Your nervous system.

Your past experiences.

Every interaction leaves a trace.

Until you change the tone.

You Don't Have to Fix the Past

Healing doesn't always mean looking back.

It means becoming a new frequency now—

and letting the old signal dissolve because it no longer matches.

You can shift your field in the present

and the memory reorganizes itself in response.

This is not theory.

This is holographic feedback.

The Field Updates to Your Tone

You don't need to revisit every wound.

You don't need to chase closure from people who aren't available.

You only need to shift your resonance.

And let the field rewire everything that was once entangled with a distorted signal.

When your signal stabilizes, timelines collapse, tension releases, stories reframe.

Not through effort.

Through coherence.

. . .

You Are a Living Echo Point

You're not just walking through life.

You're reverberating through it.

What you change inside doesn't stay inside.

It ripples into everything you've touched.

This is how collective healing begins—quietly.

One person retuning their signal becomes a stabilizing point in the web.

You don't need to understand the ripple.

You just need to initiate it.

FIELD IN MOTION

You feel guilt about a past situation and want to reach out to fix it.

Instead, pause. Hold the feeling without collapsing into it. Say: "I shift the signal now."

Breathe love and forgiveness into your own body.

That update echoes back across the connection—without a single word sent.

8
YOU ARE THE MIRROR

Everything you see is reflecting you.
Not symbolically. Mechanically.
This is a holographic reality.
Every part contains the whole.
Every moment reflects your signal.
You're not watching the world.
You're watching your field rendered into form.

What You See Is What You Broadcast
That irritating person? That's your unresolved edge.
That moment of grace? That's your coherence arriving in 3D.
You're not a passive observer.
You're an active projector.
What's around you is tuned by what's coming off of you.
Not consciously.
Energetically.

Most People React to the Screen

They try to fix the scene.
Control the image.
Change the players.
But the power's not in the screen.
It's in the source signal.
That's where reality gets rewritten.

You Don't Fix the Mirror—You Shift the Signal

When you clear resentment, triggers vanish.
When you stabilize joy, life flows around you.
When you emit clarity, the field syncs to you.
This is why inner work *works*.
Not because it's righteous.
Because it's literal.

You Are the Calibration Tool

If the scene looks off, ask:
What am I emitting?
This isn't blame.
It's ownership.
You're not causing every event.
But you're always shaping how it lands.
Always tuning what returns.

We're All Reflecting Each Other

Your clarity steadies me.
My presence tunes you.
That's not metaphor. That's resonance exchange.
You want to change the collective?
Reflect something different.
Stop reacting.
Start radiating.

Because once you see the mirror—
You can't unsee it.

FIELD IN MOTION
You catch yourself about to vent about how off everything feels. Stop mid-sentence. Ask: "What is this mirroring back to me?"

Own it without shame. Then shift your breath, your posture, your next tone.

The environment recalibrates—because it's always been listening to your signal.

9

THE DREAMER WITHIN

You're not trapped in the dream.
    You're projecting it.
    This reality is not something happening to you.
It's something happening *through* you.
Everything you see—every story, every echo, every encounter—is being rendered by consciousness.
And the projector lives inside you.

You're Not Imagining It—You're **Generating It**
You're not "making it all up."
You're tuning the field with every breath, every choice, every emotional state.
Your dreams, triggers, desires, and patterns all feed back into the hologram.
And the field mirrors it with perfect precision.
Not to punish.
To reflect.
That's how you edit the code—not with force, but with frequency.

. . .

You Are the Operator
Most people don't realize they're holding the remote.
They just keep flipping channels and calling it fate.
But when you wake up inside the dream, something shifts.
You stop reacting.
You start creating.
You realize:
The more you stabilize your tone, the more coherent the dream becomes.

You Don't Control the Dream. You Match It.
This isn't about "manifesting" on command.
It's about becoming the kind of signal the dream can align with.
You don't grab outcomes.
You broadcast the frequency they live in.
And then the field responds.
It has to.
That's how the hologram works.

You Are the Dreamer and the Dream
You're not just shaping the environment.
You *are* the environment—looping back into yourself through form.
You are the canvas and the brush.
The stage and the actor.
The signal and the story.
When you feel truth and act from it, the dream shifts.
When you collapse into fear, the feedback scrambles.
There's no judgment in that.
Just mechanics.

So Ask Yourself Clearly:

The Art of Reality:

What frequency am I projecting right now?
What version of Earth is rendering through me today?
Because every time you stabilize in truth, the illusion bends to match.

FIELD IN MOTION

You're overwhelmed and want to cancel everything—but instead you overbook your calendar to "stay productive."
That's dreaming from fear.
Pause. Say: "I'm the one projecting this pressure."
Then clear one thing off your list.
You just edited the dream in real time.

10

THE GAZE THAT CREATES

What you look at changes.
    Not just emotionally. Energetically.
    Your gaze isn't passive.
It's a selection tool.
In quantum terms:
Until you observe, a possibility remains a wave.
When you observe, it collapses into form.
But this isn't just physics.
It's your life.

Your Gaze Is a Frequency Selector
    You're not just seeing outcomes.
    You're deciding which ones become real—by how you look at them.
    If you expect chaos, you find it.
    If you look for beauty, it shows up.
    If you keep checking for failure, you reinforce its script.
    Your attention is not neutral.
    It's directive.

What you witness, you call into the timeline.

The Field Doesn't Respond to Wanting
Wanting says: "It's not here."
Trust says: "It already exists. I'm aligned with it."
The field hears that difference.
This is why vague hope rarely works.
Why desperation blocks outcomes.
Why nervous manifesting yields static.
The field doesn't sync to thought.
It syncs to the frequency behind the gaze.

What Are You Expecting?
You can say "I want peace"
But if you're still braced for the drop, the field matches your tension.
You can say "I trust love"
But if your eyes are scanning for abandonment, that's the signal being received.
This isn't punishment.
It's precision.

Witnessing Is a Technology
When you look at something with full presence—
You charge it with life.
That's why presence heals.
Why stillness shifts rooms.
Why real attention can feel like being seen for the first time.
Your gaze is a current.
You don't need to push the dream into form.
You need to *see* it clearly—without collapse, control, or clutching.
And then let the field do what it's built to do:

Respond.

FIELD IN MOTION

You're about to make a decision—but you're scanning for what might go wrong.
Pause.
Say out loud: "What I witness, I welcome."
Shift your gaze to what you actually want to reinforce.
Let that expectation settle into your body. Then act.

11

THE PROGRAM OR THE PRISM?

Are we in a simulation?
Yes—but not the kind you fear.
Not a machine.
Not a trap.
Not aliens at a console running code.
It's more elegant than that.
You are the simulation.
And you're the one programming it.

Reality Isn't Fixed—It's Fed

The field responds to frequency.
It renders what you expect, not what you prefer.
The old you—running on autopilot—lets the default code loop:
Fear. Scarcity. Control. Doubt.
The simulation keeps spinning.
But the moment you shift from unconscious to conscious transmission?
The program cracks.
And the field reshapes.

. . .

You're Not in the System. You're Emitting It.
    You're not trapped.
    You're tuned.
    You're not at the mercy of fate.
    You're broadcasting structure into space.
    You are not stuck in someone else's design.
    You are the lens bending the light.
    You are the prism.

What the System Never Told You
    It trained you to think the simulation was unchangeable.
    That you had to obey, suffer, earn, wait.
    But the truth?
    You were the creator all along.
    You just forgot.
    Because forgetting made it real.
    The veil was necessary.
    But it's thin now.
    And you're lucid.

The Prism Creates by Bending Light, Not Bracing
    When you embody truth, the simulation stops looping old code.
    It upgrades instantly.
    You don't need to escape this place.
    You need to broadcast a different tone through it.
    That's the real shift:
    You stop trying to exit the game.
    You become the one writing it from the inside.

FIELD IN MOTION

You hear bad news and brace for impact, like the spiral's about to suck you in.

Pause.

Say: "I'm not the echo. I'm the prism."

Let your body soften. Then do the next thing as if you're already free.

The code will rewrite itself around you.

12

TIME IS A CHOICE

Time isn't linear.
    It's rhythmic.
    It's not a ruler. Not a timeline. Not a law.
It's a broadcast band.
You tune it.
Or you stay trapped in its default loop.

You've Been Taught to Move Through Time
    But that's the illusion.
    You don't walk through time.
    Time moves around your signal.
    When you're locked in fear, shame, guilt—
    Time stretches.
    Delays multiply.
    Synchronicities glitch.
    But when you drop into presence—real presence—
    Time collapses.
    Things arrive.
    You land in "suddenly."

Timeline Loops Are Just Frequency Loops

You're not stuck because life is unfair.
You're stuck because your tone hasn't changed.
The future isn't waiting to unfold.
It's already there—broadcasting on a different frequency.
To get there, you don't grind.
You shift.

You Are the Tuner

Every moment, you're selecting timelines.
Not with effort. With embodiment.
When you act from coherence, you fast-forward.
When you react from the old program, you replay.
This is why some people live ten years of awakening in one year—
And others repeat the same year ten times.
Time isn't the measure.
Tone is.

This Is Why You Feel the Timeline Split

Two people on the same street.
One feels calm, aligned, intuitive.
The other feels frantic, unsafe, confused.
They're not just having different days.
They're living in different versions of time.
The split isn't coming.
It's already here.
And your nervous system is your timeline selector.

You Don't Move Toward the Future—You Match It

The version of you who has the clarity, love, peace, or creation you want?

They're not in the distance.

They're in the now—on a different frequency.

Feel them.

Embody that tone.

Choose from that state.

And time will bend.

FIELD IN MOTION

You're saying, "I'm stuck. Nothing's happening."

Pause.

Ask: "What am I still waiting for that I could embody right now?"

Breathe, and move one small action from that version of you.

That's the moment the new timeline goes live.

FIELD TECH CHECK

THE TRUTH LIVES IN YOUR FIELD

- Are you still asking for what you already are?
- Are you seeking clarity while vibrating contradiction?
- Are you calling it faith but living in default scripts?
- Are you spiritual because it's true—or because it's safer than being honest?
- Are you still performing awakening—or embodying it in quiet, frictionless ways?
- Are you using the word "God" but still imagining something separate?
- Are you waiting for permission from systems you've already outgrown?
- Are you looping for proof instead of broadcasting presence?
- Are you manifesting outcomes instead of stabilizing frequency?
- Are you mistaking urgency for purpose?

You don't need to think your way into truth.
You need to stabilize the signal.
Let your body be the answer.
Let your next action prove it.

PART II: FREQUENCY, VIBRATION & EMBODIMENT

13

EVERYTHING IS FREQUENCY

Everything is energy—
> but energy isn't the full story.
> Everything is frequency.

Not just movement. Not just buzz.
Frequency is structured signal.
It has tone, direction, coherence, and consequence.
From your thoughts to thunder, every expression in this field is vibrating at a pattern that either aligns or distorts.
And you?
You're not just made of energy.
You are frequency in form.

You Are a Signal in Motion
Your presence emits before you speak.
Your emotional state codes the room before you act.
Ever feel someone enter the space and everything tightens?
That wasn't intuition. That was frequency.
You're not just interpreting the world.
You're exchanging with it—field to field.

The Art of Reality:

What you emit is what you receive.
Not what you *want*.
What you *are*.

Your Nervous System Doesn't Lie

You can say you're fine.
But your field will broadcast anxiety, urgency, resentment, doubt—if that's what you're actually living.
This is why the field doesn't respond to language.
It responds to pattern.
High-frequency doesn't mean "positive."
It means clear.

What You Think You're Attracting Might Be What You're Reinforcing

You can want peace and still loop chaos.
You can want love and still broadcast avoidance.
Because your frequency is not your wish.
It's your felt truth.

Coherence Is the Point

Coherence doesn't mean control.
It means your body, field, and choices are all saying the same thing—without contradiction.
That's when the field locks in.
That's when timing aligns.
That's when manifestation becomes unnecessary.
Because you're no longer trying to pull something in.
You're becoming what makes it inevitable.

This Is Not About Being Happy. It's About Being Honest.

You don't need to fake light.
You need to be aligned.
You don't need to feel good.
You need to feel *what's real*—and stay present enough to broadcast from truth.

You're not here to sparkle.
You're here to stabilize.

FIELD IN MOTION

You want to attract aligned people, but you're exhausted, bracing, and saying yes when you mean no.

Stop.

Sit still. Say: "This is what my field is creating—not what I want, but what I'm tolerating."

Then make one small boundary that brings your frequency back online.

That's creation.

14

FEELINGS ARE FREQUENCY MAPS

Your feelings aren't random.
    They're directional.
    Encoded.
Alive.
Every emotion carries information.
Every sensation is a signal.
Your body isn't betraying you—it's broadcasting data.
You're not broken.
You're wired to feel your way back into alignment.

Emotion Is Field Intelligence

Most people think emotions are obstacles—something to manage, mute, escape, or explain.

But they're maps.

Each one is a pulse telling you what's off, what's rising, what's been crossed, what's ready to move.

Love expands.

Shame contracts.

Grief clears.

Anger defends.
Joy confirms.
Fear warns.
You don't need to label them "good" or "bad."
You need to feel them honestly—then translate what they're saying.

Suppression Distorts the Signal

When you numb what you feel, you disconnect from your guidance system.
When you analyze instead of inhabit, the message scrambles.
When you bypass, the field can't reorganize.
The goal is not to get over your feelings.
It's to *let them move you.*

This Is Field Literacy

Your nervous system picks up on energetic interference before your mind catches it.
You feel it in:
- The clench in your gut when something's off
- The warmth in your chest when you're seen
- The dissonance when you say yes and your body says no

That's not anxiety.
That's calibration.

Clean Frequency Doesn't Mean Calm. It Means Coherent.

You can be shaking and still clear.
You can be in grief and still radiant.
You can be angry and still aligned—if it's clean, not reactive.
Your feelings are not a liability.
They're an interface.

. . .

YOU ARE a Walking Resonance Exchange
Others feel your field before your words.
You feel theirs.
Every interaction is vibrational dialogue.
Emotional coherence sharpens your transmission.
You don't need to be emotionally perfect.
You need to be emotionally honest.

FIELD IN MOTION
You're overwhelmed, but you don't want to make it a big deal. So you brush it off, smile, keep going.
Stop.
Name the signal: "I feel pressure. Something needs attention."
Take one aligned action to release it—rest, cry, say the hard thing.
That's not weakness. That's frequency clarity in real time.

15

HEART ONLINE

The mind can track patterns.
    But only the heart can tune the field.
    You've been taught to lead with logic.
To solve, to plan, to protect.
But the real intelligence?
Lives in your chest.
The heart is not just symbolic.
It's your main signal tower.

The Heart Is Electromagnetic

It produces the strongest electrical field in your body—stronger than your brain.

It emits signal.
It shapes resonance.
It stabilizes the space around you.
When your heart is online, people feel safe before you speak.
When it's closed, the field gets scrambled.

. . .

You Were Taught to Lead from Fear
You were told to prioritize outcomes over truth.
To analyze instead of feel.
To guard instead of open.
But the heart knows before the mind catches up.
It recognizes coherence instantly.
It doesn't measure.
It remembers.

A Closed Heart Blocks the Field
When the heart is braced, nothing lands.
Truth can't enter.
Love can't stabilize.
You're stuck in reaction instead of response.
But when the heart opens—
The whole system softens.
The channel clears.
The field recalibrates.

This Isn't About Being Nice
It's about being true.
The heart doesn't avoid conflict.
It allows for connection without collapse.
This is how embodied beings lead—
Not through dominance or persuasion,
But through coherent signal that reorganizes the space around them.

Heart First. Mind in Service.
You don't need to kill your thoughts.
You need to seat them behind the heart.

When you listen from the chest, speak from the breath, and move from presence—
You're in the field.
And the field responds.

FIELD IN MOTION

You're in a conversation, but your chest is tight and your smile is fake.

Pause. Feel it.

Ask: "Is my heart online, or am I bracing?"

Drop back into your body. Loosen the armor.

Then speak one sentence from truth. Watch what shifts.

16

EARTH HAS A HEARTBEAT

You're not separate from the Earth.
　　You're patterned by her rhythm.
　　She doesn't just hold you.
She regulates you.
The Earth isn't symbolic.
She's electrical.
She's magnetic.
She's intelligent.
And she's broadcasting 24/7.

Schumann Resonance Is Real
Around 7.83 Hz.
That's Earth's natural pulse.
And it matches the frequency of calm brainwaves, deep meditation, realignment.
That's not coincidence.
It's design.
You're meant to sync with her.
You were built for it.

. . .

You Feel It—When the Static Stops
- Bare feet in the grass.
- A deep breath under trees.
- That quiet after ocean waves.
- The clarity that returns after a walk.

You don't just "feel better."
Your system is re-synchronizing.
Because your field has been blasted with distortion—
Screens. Signals. Noise.
Pace. Pressure. Performance.
Most people don't feel broken.
They feel *unregulated.*
And Earth is the original regulation device.

Get Out of Your Head. Get Into the Grid.
This isn't about "touching grass."
This is about tuning your frequency to the most ancient stabilizer available.
You want clarity?
Coherence?
Stability?
Drop in.
Touch her.
Let your signal normalize.

You're Not Visiting Nature. You Are Nature.
The idea of "escaping" to the woods or "retreating" to nature is backwards.
You're not escaping.
You're rejoining the source code.
The Earth isn't your background.

She's your motherboard.
Let her recalibrate you.

FIELD IN MOTION
You feel anxious, like your mind won't stop cycling.
Don't try to think your way out.
Go outside.
Put your bare feet on the ground. Let your skin touch something living.
That's not nature therapy. That's energetic re-alignment through Earth's code.

17

THE MUSIC OF THE SPHERES

You are not local.
You live here—but you're tuned out there.
You are built from stars, still wired to them.
The cosmos isn't silent.
It's singing.
Every planet, every star, every orbit carries frequency—
Not conceptually. Structurally.
You are not just affected by it.
You're part of the harmonic system.

THIS ISN'T ASTROLOGY. **It's Resonance.**
The ancients weren't trying to predict events.
They were listening.
They saw that the movement of celestial bodies changes the frequency field.
And you?
You're entangled with that grid.
That's why you feel the pull at full moons.
Why eclipses rearrange you.

Why Mercury retrograde scrambles your clarity.
Why a new moon feels like a reset.
It's not mystical.
It's mechanical.

Your Chart Is Your Entry Tone

Your birth chart isn't fate.
It's a frequency snapshot of your arrival.
It's the tone you walked in with.
The harmonic imprint your body remembers.
You don't have to believe in it.
You are already living it.

You're Not Separate From the Sky

The stars don't rule you.
They reflect you.
Solar flares affect your energy.
Lunar cycles regulate your body.
You are not watching the cosmos from the outside.
You are receiving its signal every second.
So stop pretending the planetary doesn't matter.
It's your mirror.

You Are a Harmonic Node

When you tune in to the cosmos, you're not being spiritual.
You're being accurate.
You are a resonator.
A living participant in the universal symphony.
To ignore that is to miss part of your own field.

FIELD IN MOTION

You feel disoriented—foggy, like time's glitching.
Instead of forcing productivity, check the rhythm.
Is the moon building? Is a planet shifting?
Adjust your pace to match the field instead of resisting it.
That's not being sensitive. That's living harmonic.

18

REFLECTIONS OF LIGHT

The Moon doesn't glow.
    It reflects.
    The Sun doesn't just shine.
It transmits.
The planets don't just orbit.
They tune the grid.
You've been taught to see the sky as a backdrop.
But it's a living interface.
You're not observing it.
You're syncing with it—every moment, whether you realize it or not.

THE MOON REGULATES Your Emotional Field
That heaviness during a full moon?
That clarity during a new one?
That tension rising as the light builds?
It's not in your head.
The Moon modulates water, cycles, tide—and your body is 70% water.

You feel it.
You just forgot what it means.

The Sun Activates **Your Codes**
The Sun isn't just light—it's data.
Photonic information, solar rhythm, circadian alignment.
When you let it hit your skin, something wakes up.
Morning light isn't just beautiful.
It resets your nervous system.
It anchors your timeline.
That feeling of *everything syncing* on a sunny day?
That's not mood.
That's biological resonance.

The Planets Are Not **Distant**
Mars ignites.
Venus harmonizes.
Saturn clarifies.
Neptune dissolves.
These aren't metaphors.
They're tones moving through the collective grid.
Astrology isn't a label.
It's a sonic map.
You don't need to worship it.
But you can work with it—if you want to stay coherent.

Tune Don't **Obey**
You don't need to track every transit.
You just need to notice how your field moves when the sky shifts.
You're not ruled.
You're informed.

This is what it means to live in relationship with the more-than-human field.

FIELD IN MOTION
You feel off and can't find the source.
Pause. Check the moon phase or where the sun is.
Is it full? Waning? Eclipse energy?
Let that reflection guide your next action—speak, rest, release, express.
The sky is not decoration. It's a tuning fork.

19

INTENT IS THE ENGINE

Intent is not a wish.
It's a direction encoded with frequency.
More than hope.
More than clarity.
Intent is a signal you anchor—consciously or not—every time you move, speak, decide, or hesitate.
And it tells the field exactly how to respond.

You're Always Broadcasting Something
Even when you say, "I don't know what I want"—that's an intent.
Confusion is a tone.
Avoidance is a tone.
Fear is a tone.
And the field isn't listening to your words.
It's following your energetic command.

Intent Isn't Force. It's Coherence

Intent is not controlling outcomes.

It's aligning your state, your signal, and your decision into one undivided broadcast.

The clearer the intent, the cleaner the response.

The fuzzier the tone, the more distorted the return.

Intent = direction + embodiment.

That's what the field hears.

HALF-INTENT DELIVERS HALF-RESULTS

If part of you wants it, but part of you doesn't trust it?

That's not intent.

That's static.

The signal becomes unstable.

Reality reflects the fragmentation.

WANT TO COLLAPSE A TIMELINE? Set the Tone, Then Let Go

You don't need to micromanage.

You need to transmit with stability.

Intent is the seed.

The field organizes around that.

Say it.

Feel it.

Live like it's already in motion.

Then stop gripping.

This isn't detachment—it's energetic integrity.

You're not hoping.

You've already chosen.

FIELD IN MOTION

You keep saying you want clarity, but your actions show hesitation.

Pause.

Speak your real intent aloud: "I'm ready to see the next clear step."

Feel it in your body. Then move—anywhere—even if small.

The field needs that signal to begin building around you.

20

TUNE UP

You don't raise your frequency by pretending to be okay.
You raise it by becoming honest, clear, and present.
This isn't about "high vibes."
This is about signal clarity.
Your frequency is not your mood.
It's your total field tone—how your breath, thoughts, body, voice, and choices align.
Every moment is an opportunity to tune.
Not to be better—just clearer.

The Field Doesn't Care If You're Smiling

You can be crying and still high frequency—if you're aligned.
You can be cheerful and still distorted—if you're hiding.
Clarity has nothing to do with appearance.
It's about whether your internal tone is integrated.
That's the real shift.

. . .

You Don't Need to Feel Better. You Need to Feel Truth.
Stop chasing a mood.
Start anchoring your signal.
What tunes you isn't performance.
It's precision.

How to Tune Your Frequency
Not everything works every time.
The point isn't the method—it's the match.
Try:
- **Stillness.** Let the real tone surface.
- **Movement.** Shake, stretch, sweat—let energy move out.
- **Breath.** Slow, long exhales recalibrate faster than thoughts.
- **Sound.** Hum, sing, listen. Let the resonance clear static.
- **Nature.** Let the Earth retune you without effort.
- **Gratitude.** Not as a checklist—just a felt moment of enoughness.
- **Truth.** Speak it. Write it. Even whisper it. But don't deny it.

You don't need all of them.
Just one. Done fully.

Frequency Is Choice in Motion
Tuning isn't about perfection.
It's about awareness.
Feel off? Don't spiral.
Just pause. Breathe. Re-center.
Your tone is not a mystery.
It's a choice.
And when you shift it, reality shifts too.

FIELD IN MOTION

You feel reactive, ungrounded, scattered—but you keep pushing through.

Stop.

Step away for 3 minutes. Put a hand on your chest. Breathe deep. Hum. Stretch. Name what you're avoiding.

Then return—but from your signal, not your scramble.

21

WHAT THEY CALL 'HIGH VIBE' IS OFTEN JUST FEAR IN DISGUISE

You don't need to raise your frequency.
You need to clear it.
A lot of what's called "high vibe" is actually just fear—with better marketing.
Smiling when you want to cry.
Saying "love and light" instead of naming the truth.
Telling yourself you've transcended something just to avoid feeling it.
That's not mastery.
That's bypass.

This Isn't About Being Light. It's About Being Clear.
You're not here to float above distortion.
You're here to become so anchored in your tone that distortion can't stick to you.
That doesn't mean you're calm all the time.
It means you're *coherent*.
You can be furious and still in alignment.
You can be grieving and still powerful.

You can be silent and still broadcasting truth.
That's frequency integrity.

Spiritual Image Is Still **Programming**
It's just wearing linen.
If you're afraid to be messy, human, or contradictory—
That's not spiritual evolution.
That's conditioning with a new costume.
Real clarity doesn't require polish.
It requires presence.

Don't Rise Above It. Drop In.
You don't need to elevate your energy.
You need to stop leaking it by performing what you think alignment should look like.
Drop the pose.
Drop the script.
Feel what's actually alive.
Then move from there.
That's the real "high" frequency: undistorted honesty.

FIELD IN MOTION
You feel off, but you tell someone, "I'm good!" out of habit.
Pause.
Say instead: "I'm a little scattered, actually."
Watch how fast your body relaxes when you stop pretending.
That's frequency coming back online.

22

THE FIELD DELIVERS WHEN YOU STOP GRIPPING

You were taught to manifest through force.
   Visualize harder.
   Say the affirmations.
Write the script. Check the vision board.
That's not manifestation.
That's tension.
And tension distorts your signal.

The Field Doesn't Respond to Effort. It Responds to Certainty.
   Wanting says: "It's not here."
   Gripping says: "It won't come unless I force it."
   Both send static.
   The field doesn't organize around need.
   It organizes around tone.
   And the tone of surrender—done cleanly, not passively—is magnetic.

You're Not Waiting. You're Matching.

You don't call in what you want.
You *become* the version of you that already holds it.
Then you move like it's already locked in—without obsession.
This is not about letting go of your desire.
It's about letting go of your fear.

SURRENDER ISN'T WEAK. **It's Instructional.**
When you stop refreshing your energetic inbox, you tell the field:
"I trust the signal I already sent."
And that's when things move.
Because you finally made space.

MANIFESTATION WITHOUT COHERENCE **Is Just Delay.**
You don't need to prove anything.
You don't need to hustle clarity.
You don't need to micro-control the how.
You need to emit a stable field, act from alignment, and *let it arrive how it needs to.*
This is how the field works.
It doesn't reward want.
It matches state.

FIELD IN MOTION
You keep checking your inbox, wondering why your opportunity hasn't come.
Pause.
Say, "It's already in motion. I don't chase what's mine."
Go do something that makes you feel already met—rest, create, walk, play.
That's not detachment. That's making room for delivery.

FIELD TECH CHECK

Your Signal Is Showing

- Are you present in your body, or are you managing your image?
    - Are you calling it peace, or have you just shut down emotion?
    - Are you grounding with the Earth—or with your routine?
    - Are your words clean, or coded with hidden asks?
    - Are you using "I'm fine" to avoid feeling what's true?
    - Is your creativity coming from pressure or pulse?
    - Are you mistaking tension for alignment?
    - Are you feeling your field—or thinking about it?
    - Are you acting from coherence—or reacting from conditioning?
    - Are you performing the signal—or living it?

The field doesn't need your perfection.
It needs your precision.
Feel what's real.
Move from there.
That's embodiment.

PART III: ACTIVATION & ALIGNMENT

23

REWRITE THE CODE, REWIRE THE FIELD

Your subconscious isn't hidden.
 It's humming underneath everything—silently running your field.
You're not creating reality from your thoughts.
You're creating from your *patterns*—most of which were installed before you had a choice.

Old Code Is Just Old Frequency
That constant self-doubt?
That impulse to apologize for existing?
That fear of being too much or not enough?
That's not personality.
That's programming.
Most of your field is still running code inherited from childhood, culture, lineage, trauma.
It's not your fault.
But now that you're aware—it's your responsibility.

. . .

The Subconscious Isn't Deep. It's Just Rehearsed.

It's not hiding. It's looping.

And your job isn't to find every root—it's to stop feeding the old signal.

Rewriting doesn't require analysis.

It requires *interruption*.

Catch the loop. Pause. Choose differently.

Every time you do, the field updates.

How to Rewrite

You don't fix the old self.

You install the new one.

Here's how:

- **Speak a new truth**—not as a mantra, but as a frequency you feel.
- **Move your body differently**—your posture stores memory.
- **Breathe into the future you**—as if it's already lived.
- **Feel coherence** before proof shows up. That's the rewrite.
- **Sleep in the new tone.** Drift off while transmitting the version of you you're becoming.

This is not delusion.

It's field leadership.

You Are the Interface

Your beliefs are code.

Your body is the keyboard.

Your breath is the send button.

You don't need to clear everything.

You need to *transmit something new long enough* for the field to reorganize.

And it will.

Because the field is listening.

. . .

FIELD IN MOTION
    You notice the old pattern: hesitation, apology, retreat.
    Pause.
    Say aloud: "That code is old. I'm running something else now."
    Straighten your spine. Move like it's already updated.
    That's not pretending. That's frequency override.

24

LIVING MEDITATION, MOVING FREQUENCY

Meditation isn't something you do.
    It's a way of being.
    You've been taught that presence requires stillness—
    A cushion, a timer, a technique.
    But real meditation begins when the bell ends.
    It's not silence.
    It's signal clarity.

MEDITATION MEANS Your Field Leads the Room
    It's when your breath steadies the space.
    When your eyes soften the noise.
    When your presence untangles distortion without effort.
    That doesn't happen just because you sat for 20 minutes.
    It happens when your awareness keeps transmitting—through walking, speaking, listening, creating, resting.
    That's meditation: embodied coherence in motion.

. . .

Stillness Is Not the Only Entry Point
Presence doesn't mean freezing.
It means not leaking.
You can be in motion and still anchored.
You can be talking and still in deep transmission.
You don't have to be still to be clear.
You just have to stop splitting your energy.

The Field Reads How You Move
How you stir your coffee.
How you respond to an interruption.
How you listen without rushing to speak.
Every motion is a broadcast.
This is meditation without a brand.
This is practice without performance.

Want to Live as Meditation? Try This:
- Breathe before you speak.
- Walk like your body is leading, not your mind.
- Do one task with full attention—no split screen.
- Feel what's here now, not what might happen next.
- Let your nervous system set the pace—not your fear of being late.

When you stop abandoning the moment, the moment bends toward you.

FIELD IN MOTION
You're rushing through your day, jumping from task to task.
Stop.
Pick one thing—pouring tea, folding clothes, washing your face.
Do it slowly. Fully.

Let your body be the transmitter, not your thoughts.
That's meditation in motion.

25

RECEIVE THE LIGHT, REMEMBER THE CODE

The Sun is not just warmth.
    It's information.
    The stars are not just distant.
They're transmitters.
Light isn't symbolic.
It's coded.
It delivers frequency directly into your field.
And when you receive it consciously—
You remember.

Photonic Light Carries Blueprint Activation
When you expose your body to natural light—especially early morning sunlight or star glow—something wakes up.
It's not mental.
It's not mystical.
It's signal integration.
Light interacts with your DNA.
With your nervous system.

With your memory.
It reboots what's been dormant.

This Is Why Some Moments Crack You Open
That sunset that made you cry.
That golden glow that made everything feel like home.
That starry night that made you still.
Those weren't emotional reactions.
They were activations.
The field was delivering something your body already knew.

Light Doesn't Need Your Understanding. It Needs Your Openness.
You don't need to interpret the feeling.
You don't need to name the code.
You just need to receive it.
Lie in the sun.
Look at the stars.
Let your body recalibrate without explaining anything.
This is cellular awakening—not strategy.

The Stars Carry Your Origin Point
Every being has a stellar lineage.
You're not from "now."
You're from pattern, light, and tone.
When you gaze into the sky, your field remembers its entry code.
You feel small—but expansive.
That's alignment.

FIELD IN MOTION

You feel fragmented, like your body and mind are out of sync.

Go outside. Close your eyes.

Let the sun hit your face, or look up at the stars without asking for meaning.

Breathe.

Let the light recalibrate what words can't reach.

26

THE EYE THAT REMEMBERS

You've been seeing with two eyes.
    But there was always a third.
    Not as a metaphor.
As a system.
The pineal gland isn't spiritual poetry.
It's literal hardware.
It's the receiver.
The tuner.
The lens between visible form and vibrational truth.

Your First Eye—Not Your Third

The pineal was active before the world trained you to ignore it.
It remembers what your mind forgot:
Pattern.
Symbol.
Signal.
Coherence.
When it's online, you don't just believe truth—you see it.
Not visually.

Energetically.

This Eye Doesn't Look for Proof. It Feels the Signal.
You walk into a room and know what's off.
You hear someone speak and sense what's unsaid.
You read between timelines.
You decode pattern in silence.
That's not intuition.
That's resonance through the lens of coherence.

Clarity Isn't a Superpower. It's Sight Restored.
Your pineal doesn't open through crystals or effort.
It opens through purity of tone.
Static dulls it:
- Fluoride
- Fear
- Chronic overstimulation
- Disconnection from nature
- Mental loops

Clear your field, and clarity returns.
Your cells aren't just biological—they're vibrational.
Inside each one, your mitochondria act like tuning amplifiers.
They don't just power your body.
They respond to light, memory, and frequency.

When you receive solar light or activate inner coherence, your mitochondria signal across the entire system.

This isn't woo—it's bioelectric clarity.

Your field gets sharper when your cells remember how to communicate.

You Were Never Blind. Just Distracted.
This eye has been waiting.

And once it activates?
Your discernment sharpens.
Your illusions fall away.
You stop second-guessing.
Because you *feel the shape of truth* before it forms.

FIELD IN MOTION
Someone's words sound nice, but your body feels off.
Don't override it.
Say internally: "My eye sees what's true."
Let your actions follow that frequency—not the story.
That's discernment leading vision.

27

MOVE THE ENERGY, WAKE THE CODES

Your body isn't a container.
It's a conductor.
Every joint, every breath, every tremble—alive with signal.
Not just sensation.
Memory.
Code.
Movement isn't optional.
It's how the system clears static, rewrites pattern, and reactivates stored wisdom.

Stagnation Is a Signal, **Not a Failure**
If you feel stuck, heavy, unclear—don't overthink it.
Your field is asking for movement.
Not hustle. Not performance.
Just motion.
Because emotion, memory, trauma, and light codes are all stored in tissue.
And when energy doesn't move, distortion accumulates.

. . .

YOU DON'T NEED CHOREOGRAPHY. You Need Presence.
- Shake.
- Sway.
- Stretch.
- Run.
- Dance.
- Crawl.
- Lay on the floor and breathe until the next gesture arrives.

You're not trying to perform healing.
You're allowing the body to *finish what the field already knows.*

THE BODY HAS BEEN HOLDING the Loop
Your hips carry unsaid truth.
Your throat protects what wasn't safe to speak.
Your spine remembers every time you braced instead of broke open.
You don't need to fix it.
You need to move it.
When you move with awareness, you invite release.
You change the grid—not with language, but with posture.

MOVEMENT IS NOT A DETOUR. It's the Code Key.
This is why the ancients danced.
Why warriors practiced forms.
Why shamans trembled, spiraled, chanted.
Because motion *is* remembering.
You are the ritual.
The activation.
The initiator.

. . .

FIELD IN MOTION

You feel stuck at your desk, foggy, frustrated.

Stand up. Shake your limbs. Breathe loud. Move like the pattern is leaving through your fingertips.

Don't wait to understand—just let it go.

That's not dramatic. That's release.

28

THE POWER OF COHERENCE

You don't need more effort.
You need a cleaner signal.
Everyone talks about energy, vibration, manifestation—
But few talk about the real thing that shifts reality:
Coherence.
Coherence is when every part of you is saying the same thing.
No split signal. No static. No leak.

Coherence Isn't About Perfection. **It's About Precision.**
It's when your words, choices, breath, body, and actions all point in the same direction—without hidden fear, grasping, or contradiction.
You can be in pain and still coherent.
You can be quiet and still powerful.
You can be simple and still commanding.
Because coherence doesn't come from appearance.
It comes from integrity.

. . .

The Field Reads Coherence Before Anything Else
Not your mood.
Not your "vision."
Not how spiritual you sound.
The field picks up your alignment before you open your mouth.
It organizes around your clarity—or reflects your scramble.

Where You Leak, You Loop
Mixed messages create delay.
You say you trust, but your body braces.
You act peaceful, but you're seething underneath.
You speak truth, but then soften it to avoid discomfort.
That's not alignment.
That's performance.
Coherence means owning the whole signal.

You Don't Need to Be Perfect—You Need to Be Honest
This isn't about always being calm.
It's about being real.
Coherence means:
- No inner betrayal
- No energetic apology
- No broadcasting "yes" when your field says "no"

It's not rigid.
It's clear.
And clarity is the tone that moves timelines.

Coherence Is Everything
Not a part of the process.
Not a bonus.
Not an ideal.
It is the entire mechanism.

Reality doesn't shift because you try.
It shifts because your field becomes undeniable.
This is why half-truths collapse.
Why performing alignment never lasts.
Why the moment you stabilize your real tone—without distortion—
everything around you starts to move.
Because coherence isn't just power.
It is the frequency the field was built to follow.

FIELD IN MOTION

You're about to say yes—but your chest tightens and your throat goes quiet.

Pause.

Say nothing. Feel everything.

Then respond from the signal, not the script.

That one clean act of coherence will shift more than a hundred polite agreements.

29

BECOME THE CURRENT

Flow is not a mood.
It's a dimension.
You don't enter it by thinking.
You enter it by *becoming it*.
Flow isn't the absence of effort.
It's the absence of resistance.
When you're in it, time bends.
Ideas arrive.
Your body leads.
You stop checking. You start channeling.
That's not magic.
That's frequency alignment in motion.

Flow Is What Happens When You Stop Interrupting the Signal
It doesn't require a special state.
It requires the removal of static.
What blocks flow?
- Overanalyzing

- Bracing
- Controlling outcomes
- Trying to "get it right" before moving

None of that is clarity.

It's just delay.

You Don't Need More Confidence. You Need Less Interference.

You don't need a plan.

You need permission to act from presence.

When you follow the current of your own signal, momentum builds.

When you grip the wheel too hard, nothing moves.

Flow Isn't Passive. It's Precision in Motion.

You can't fake it.

You can't force it.

But you *can* become it—by aligning your state, then acting from there.

Flow is honest energy expressed without apology.

It's movement without collapse.

It's coherence with momentum.

You Are Not the Observer Anymore. You Are the Current.

The days of watching yourself from the outside are over.

Step in.

Feel the rhythm.

Move as the signal.

That's how timelines bend—by being lived, not visualized.

FIELD IN MOTION

You get a creative hit, but second-guess it and scroll instead.
Catch it.
Say: "This is the moment."
Act immediately—start the sketch, send the message, hit record.

That's what becoming the current looks like: no gap between impulse and movement.

30

JOY IS A FREQUENCY CODE

Joy isn't extra.
    It's essential.
    It's not what happens after you heal.
    It's the sign that your field is running clear.
Joy is not a personality trait.
It's not a reward for doing life right.
It's signal confirmation:
"You're aligned. Keep going."

Joy Isn't Always Loud
    Sometimes it's a tingle.
    Sometimes it's a calm sense of yes.
    Sometimes it's the moment you stop bracing and just breathe.
    Joy isn't about happiness.
    It's about *energetic permission*.
    When it shows up, it means the distortion just dropped.
    And your real tone came back online.

· · ·

You Were Taught to Mistrust It
You were taught to distrust your delight.
To postpone joy until work is done.
To view it as a luxury or a weakness.
But your field knows better.
Excitement is your compass.
Laughter is nervous system coherence.
Play is pattern release.
Joy is *truth showing up through sensation.*

You Don't Have to Earn It. You Just Stop Blocking It.
When your frequency is clean—joy finds you.
When you stop bracing, the current lifts.
When you stop proving, the pleasure returns.
You don't generate joy.
You allow it.
And when you stabilize it, timelines collapse in your favor.
Not because joy is powerful—
but because it's proof you stopped pretending.

FIELD IN MOTION
You feel light, clear, suddenly at ease—but you question it, thinking it's not "productive."
Pause.
Say: "This is joy. This is truth."
Let yourself stay in it without looking for the catch.
That's not a distraction. That's alignment doing its job.

31

CREATION IS A CHANNEL

Art isn't decoration.
 It's delivery.
  You're not just making something.
You're receiving something.
And sending it back.
When you create from alignment, you become a channel—not for ideas, but for signal.

Creativity Is Field Movement
The best work doesn't come from brainstorming.
It arrives when your field opens.
You feel the current.
Your hands start moving.
You follow it.
You don't edit too soon.
You let it speak through you.
That's not inspiration.
That's broadcast.

. . .

YOU ARE NOT THE SOURCE. You Are the Transmitter.
>The ego wants to take credit.
>But real creation humbles you.
>It moves through your body with a logic you didn't invent.
>Your role is to get out of the way—
>And stay present enough to carry the signal clearly.

YOU DON'T HAVE to Understand What You're Making
>You don't need a plan.
>You need openness.
>The medium doesn't matter:
>- A sound
>- A gesture
>- A sentence
>- A garden
>- A dance
>- A decision
>
>If it came through resonance, it's real.

MAKE What Moves You Before You Name It
>Don't wait to be certain.
>Start moving. Start shaping.
>The transmission refines itself *through expression*.
>Creation isn't what you do.
>It's what you let through.

FIELD IN MOTION
>You feel something stirring but hesitate because it doesn't make sense yet.
>Pause.
>Pick up the pen. Open the voice memo. Begin the gesture.

Let it come through without labeling it.
That's not premature—that's how the code enters the field.

32

CHOOSE THE DOOR, ACTIVATE THE PATH

Awakening doesn't have one path.
It has a thousand doors.
The question isn't, "Am I on the right path?"
It's, "Did I walk through the door that just opened?"
Your signal will always show you the next entry point.
The only thing required is your response.

The Invitation Is Always Here

Sometimes the door looks like chaos.
Sometimes like silence.
Sometimes like beauty so strong it breaks you open.
It could be:
- A pattern resurfacing
- A relationship ending
- A truth you can't unsee
- A body signal you finally stop ignoring

That's not distraction.
That's the activation.

. . .

You Don't Need Permission to Walk Through

You don't need to understand it yet.
You don't need credentials.
You don't need to explain.
You just need to say:
"Yes. This is the signal. I'm responding."
That's how the path reveals itself—*through alignment, not certainty.*

Stop Waiting to Feel Ready

The path doesn't ask if you're prepared.
It asks if you're *listening*.
Awakening isn't linear.
It spirals.
Each time the invitation returns, it meets a clearer version of you.
That's not backsliding. That's mastery.

The Activation Lives in Response

Every time you:
- Set a boundary
- Speak a small truth
- Move toward a desire without a map
- Rest when you'd usually perform
- Follow the quiet yes

You open the next field layer.
There are no missing steps.
Only missed responses.

FIELD IN MOTION

You feel the tug to shift something—but you hesitate, waiting for confirmation.
Pause.

Ask: "Is this my door?"

If your body says yes, act—even if it's small.

That's how the path activates: not through answers, but through movement.

33
FIELD TECH CHECK

ALIGNED ACTION REWRITES REALITY

- Are you listening to what's actually opening—or waiting for something more dramatic?
  - Are you chasing the big purpose while ignoring the small yes?
  - Are you doing what's expected—or what's encoded?
  - Are you acting from alignment—or waiting for proof?
  - Are you over-preparing to avoid uncertainty?
  - Are you checking the signs—or feeling the signal?
  - Are you treating your body like a partner—or a servant?
  - Are you waiting for external validation—or activating internal direction?
  - Are you looping lessons—or stepping into embodiment?
  - Are you holding the vision—or walking as it?

The path isn't something you find.
It's something you choose—again and again.
Walk through the next door.

Let it show you who you are now.

PART IV: SACRED SIGNAL AND HUMAN FIELD

34

THE BODY REMEMBERS LIGHT

You're not disconnected.
   You're overloaded.
   You're not broken.
You're broadcasting loops.
The body isn't resisting healing.
It's waiting for your signal to become coherent enough to receive it.
You don't need fixing.
You need remembering.

Your Body Holds the Original Blueprint
   Your cells haven't forgotten.
   Your field hasn't either.
   It remembers what it felt like to be whole.
   To be uncollapsed.
   To be fully online.
   The memory of light isn't metaphorical.
   It's embedded in your structure—waiting to be reactivated.

. . .

The Answers Are Not Outside You
No method. No healer. No system holds your source code.
You already came with it.
Every time you ask someone else what to do,
every time you delay by seeking more information,
you postpone the moment your body has been ready for.
You don't need more guidance.
You need to trust your own frequency when it starts to stir.

The Field Doesn't Need Perfection. It Needs Your Attention.
Your shoulder tension isn't a flaw.
Your gut ache isn't sabotage.
Your heart racing isn't drama.
It's data.
It's signal.
It's memory rising to the surface for review and reconfiguration.
You don't need to decode it all.
You just need to feel it clearly and stop overriding it.

Every Sensation Is a Messenger
Your nervous system isn't betraying you.
It's informing you.
Your bones hold the hum of ancient tone.
Your fascia is wired for memory.
Your breath carries electromagnetic intention.
When you stop numbing and start listening,
you remember your original broadcast.
And the field remembers with you.

FIELD IN MOTION
You feel a tension rise and your first instinct is to get busy, get distracted, or fix it.

Pause.

Put a hand on the area. Ask: "What are you trying to tell me?"
Breathe there. Let it speak through sensation—not words.
That's not delay. That's the healing happening.

35

THE BODY IS A SYMPHONY

You are not just a body.
    You are an instrument of frequency—wired for tone, resonance, and response.
Every part of you vibrates.
Every organ, cell, and system has a natural pitch.
When aligned, they harmonize.
When distorted, they create internal dissonance.
Your job isn't to fix the sound.
It's to *listen to it*.

You Don't Just Feel **Music. You Are Music.**
    You know this.
That moment when a sound makes your skin exhale.
When a song breaks your heart open without warning.
When silence buzzes louder than noise.
That's not emotion.
That's your field remembering harmony.

. . .

Your Body Is Tuned by Sound

The right vibration can:
- Dissolve stored trauma
- Regulate your nervous system
- Activate dormant codes
- Reconnect you to your original signal

You don't need to understand how.
You need to *let it move you.*

Each Layer Has a Role

- **Bones** carry deep structural tone
- **Organs** pulse unique rhythms
- **Fascia** acts as connective wiring
- **Voice** broadcasts intention
- **Breath** modulates energy
- **Skin** listens to vibration

You're not a mechanical machine.
You're a harmonic system.

Sound Is a Shortcut to Coherence

Toning, humming, singing, shaking, listening in stillness—these are not silly or indulgent.

They are field tools.
Frequency reset buttons.
Truth locators.
Let yourself sound.
Let yourself be sounded.

FIELD IN MOTION

You feel tight in your chest and try to journal your way through it.
Stop.

Close your eyes. Hum gently into your body. Let the sound land where the tension lives.

Keep going until something softens, cracks, or moves.

That's your inner symphony tuning itself back into harmony.

36

THE SPIRAL REMEMBERS

You were never walking a straight line.
　　　You were spiraling.
　　　Healing. Returning. Re-seeing.
The spiral is not metaphor.
It's memory made visible.
It's the native shape of evolution.
DNA moves in spirals.
Galaxies spin.
Your fingerprints curve.
You weren't meant to move forward.
You were meant to move *through*.

You're Not Repeating. You're Refining.
　　You don't come back to the same pattern because you failed.
　　You come back with new eyes.
　　New tone.
　　New clarity.
　　Every return is an opportunity to choose differently.

The Art of Reality:

To witness without collapse.
To hold the thread instead of knotting it again.
That's not regression.
That's integration.

The Spiral Holds Grace

It doesn't punish.
It repatterns.
It brings you back around to reclaim the parts of you still hiding.
Every ache that resurfaces isn't a setback.
It's a checkpoint.
"Are you ready to walk this moment as the real you?"

You're Not Behind. You're Becoming Precise.

The spiral teaches depth, not speed.
It asks for presence over progress.
It brings wisdom through rhythm, not performance.
It softens the edges of the past until they release their grip.
It gives you a chance to carry the same situation in a new tone.

Let the Spiral Teach You Time

Stop looking for the straight path.
Start looking at how your field wants to unwind.
Let the spiral become your compass.
Let it show you that the return is the revelation.

FIELD IN MOTION

You catch yourself in a familiar loop—same fear, same trigger, same reaction.
Don't shame it.

Pause and say, "This is the spiral. I've been here before, but I'm different now."

Respond one breath slower. One tone clearer.

That's the spiral completing a layer—not looping endlessly.

37

THE BEAUTIFUL FIELD

The Field isn't just energy.
    It's intelligence.
        Alive. Organized. Responsive.
And when it's undistorted, it expresses as beauty.
Not aesthetic.
Not perfection.
Beauty is how truth feels when it lands.

The Field Doesn't Judge. It Mirrors.
    It reflects your broadcast in exact, fractal precision.
    If your inner signal is clear, the outer world softens.
    If your signal is split, the world gets noisy.
    This isn't punishment.
    It's feedback.
    The Field isn't withholding from you.
    It's waiting for you to come back into coherence.

. . .

You Don't Attract What You Want. You Attract What You Are.

Not what you say.
Not what you hope.
What you stabilize.
That's how the Field responds.

Beauty Is the Signature of Resonance

When your thoughts become beautiful—not pleasing, but honest—
the Field rearranges around them.
- A bird sings in perfect timing.
- A stranger smiles with a frequency you recognize.
- Light falls in a way that reminds you you're not separate.

You didn't create those moments.
You remembered them into view.

Stop Trying to Manipulate the Field. Let It Love You Back into Alignment.

When your field returns to truth, life responds with beauty.
Not decoration.
Design.
Not effort.
Harmony.
The more you emit clarity, the more the Field surrounds you with signals of yes.
This isn't control.
It's communion.

FIELD IN MOTION

You walk into a space and feel off—chaotic, unwelcoming, noisy.
Pause.

Breathe. Let your body return to stillness. Don't fight the energy —clean yours.

Notice how something shifts around you without you saying a word.

That's the Field answering resonance with beauty.

38

THE SPIRAL CODE

There's a reason the ancients carved spirals into stone.
    They weren't decorating.
    They were documenting the architecture of the field.
The spiral is not symbolic.
It's instructive.
It's how light moves.
How memory unfolds.
How form organizes itself in space and time.
You're not linear.
You're spiral-coded.

YOU WERE NEVER MEANT to Move Straight
    The spiral curves, winds, and returns—
    But always at a higher octave.
    It brings you back to the same point with more awareness.
    Same theme, different tone.
    Same situation, new choice.
    This is not regression.

This is frequency refinement.

Every Spiral Loop Is a Recoding Opportunity
Each return carries potential:
- Revisit the wound with compassion
- Re-enter the pattern with boundary
- Re-meet the fear with breath
- Reframe the memory with coherence

The spiral doesn't trap you.
It tunes you.

You Don't Just Walk the Spiral. You Become It.
When you stop resisting the return, you start shaping the spiral intentionally.

Every movement, pause, release, and rise becomes part of the waveform.

You shift the field not by escaping it—but by *reorganizing your place within it.*

This is sacred geometry made flesh.

Let the Spiral Be Your Teacher
Stop asking, "Why am I here again?"
Start asking, "How can I walk this with more presence?"
That's when you exit repetition.
And enter conscious creation.

FIELD IN MOTION
You feel frustrated: "Why am I dealing with this again?"
Pause.
Say: "This is a spiral, not a setback."

Then make one new micro-choice—one small upgrade to your tone or timing.

That's the Spiral Code completing a pattern instead of looping it.

39

THE BODY REMEMBERS THE FIELD

You don't just walk through the Field.
You are the Field—made visible.
Every part of your body holds signal.
Every tension, twitch, ache, or wave is communication.
This isn't metaphor.
It's how the system works.
You don't "tap into" wisdom.
You *embody* it.

THE FIELD DOESN'T FORGET. **Your Body Is Echoing It.**
That knot in your throat?
That pang in your chest?
That tightness in your jaw?
That's not random.
That's stored resonance waiting to complete its loop.
The Field remembers.
And your body is the interface that brings it back online.

. . .

You Are a Living Broadcast
>   Every movement is a message.
>   Every breath is a recalibration.
>   Every sensation is signal trying to reach you.
>   Stop translating everything into words.
>   Start feeling the instruction inside the sensation.

Your Body Isn't a Problem. It's a Pattern You're Meant to Read.
>   You've been trained to ignore it, drug it, numb it, silence it.
>   But that ache is information.
>   That tightness is memory.
>   That breathlessness is your tone out of sync.
>   When you listen with presence instead of panic,
>   the energy reorganizes itself.

You Don't Heal Through Force. You Realign Through Attention.
>   The moment you feel without fixing, the loop can close.
>   The charge can release.
>   The timeline can shift.
>   You're not feeling "too much."
>   You're finally hearing clearly.

FIELD IN MOTION

You get a sudden wave of emotion or tightness. You go to override it with action.

Stop.

Ask: "What field am I echoing right now?"

Breathe into the sensation. Let it speak.

Respond from that clarity—not from your script.

That's how the Field moves through the body and out into new form.

40

THE SIGNAL BEYOND THE SIGNAL

There's the message.
    And then—there's the signal beneath it.
    The tone.
The tension.
The vibration behind the voice.
That's what you're actually responding to.
Not the words.
The frequency they're riding on.

Words Can Lie. Tone Can't.
    Someone says "I'm fine," but your body clenches.
    Someone says "I love you," but it lands flat.
    Someone says "You're safe," and you feel braced anyway.
    That's not you being sensitive.
    That's you being accurate.
    You're reading the signal beyond the signal.
    Because the Field doesn't respond to language.
    It responds to *coherence*.

. . .

You Can't Performance-Pitch the Field

You can say all the right things and still broadcast confusion, control, or fear.

You can quote truth and still leak desperation.

You can smile while transmitting collapse.

The Field doesn't care about how polished you sound.

It listens to what you *are*.

Real Presence Carries Clarity

When you stop trying to convince,

when you stop diluting to be liked,

when you stop managing perception—

your tone stabilizes.

And in that moment, your presence starts to do the work your words never could.

You Are the Transmission

True energetic leadership doesn't come from teaching.

It comes from walking into the room with nothing hidden.

Clean tone.

No scramble.

No hidden ask.

That's the real signal.

And it moves people before they know why.

FIELD IN MOTION

You're about to share something vulnerable, but your voice is tight and your breath shallow.

Pause.

Say: "Am I speaking to connect, or to control the reaction?"

Adjust your breath. Drop your tone into truth.

Let the signal speak for itself—before the words even arrive.

41

EMBODIMENT IS THE ANSWER

You've read enough.
    You've listened enough.
    You've asked enough.
Now it's time to walk it.
Because embodiment is not a phase.
It's the point.
You don't become free through ideas.
You become free through integration.

Your Body Is the Place Where Truth Lands
    Not in your thoughts.
    Not in your performance.
    In your walk.
    In your tone.
    In your stillness.
    If it's not living in your body,
    it's not integrated yet.
    And that's not judgment.

That's just signal honesty.

This Isn't About Being Calm. It's About Being Here.
Can you speak your truth without bracing?
Can you listen without reacting?
Can you breathe while being seen?
That's embodiment.

You Don't Need Another Layer of Insight. You Need to Move Differently.
Every time you act from coherence—even in small, boring, invisible ways—
you collapse old timelines.
Because what shifts the Field isn't performance.
It's *presence*.

Stop Looking for a Way Out. Drop All the Way In.
You don't need to rise.
You need to land.
Land in your breath.
Land in your body.
Land in the moment where your nervous system stops outsourcing authority.
This is where truth lives now.
Not above.
In.

FIELD IN MOTION
You're feeling the truth but waiting for the right moment to live it.
Pause.

Ask: "Can I let this truth take shape in my posture, my tone, my next move?"

Do it now—even subtly.

That's embodiment. Not idea. Action. Presence. Signal.

42

THE END OF MANIFESTATION AS A PRACTICE

You don't need to manifest.
    Not like that.
    Not with rituals.
Not with scripting.
Not with forced clarity and mental control.
You're not here to prove to the universe you're ready.
You are the universe—expressed as a stable field.
You don't need to call things in.
You need to *become the signal they already respond to*.

MANIFESTATION ISN'T Something You Do. It's Something You Allow.
    If you're still chasing outcomes,
    you're not manifesting.
    You're gripping.
    And gripping is just fear in performance mode.

YOUR REALITY ISN'T WAITING. It's Mirroring.

The Art of Reality:

Whatever you stabilize, you live.
Whatever you leak, you delay.
Whatever you embody fully—*without wobble*—arrives on time.
The field doesn't respond to effort.
It responds to resonance.

THE FIELD DOESN'T NEED CONVINCING

You don't need to visualize harder.
You don't need to say the affirmation 55 times.
You need to:
- Align with the tone
- Act from the timeline
- And stop refreshing the energetic inbox

When your field says "done,"
life reorganizes around that statement.

STABILIZATION REPLACES STRATEGY

Your nervous system is the signal.
Your coherence is the portal.
Your stillness is the manifestation tool.
You're not attracting.
You're matching.

FIELD IN MOTION

You want to "call something in," so you light a candle and do your ritual.
But underneath, you're still doubting it will work.
Pause.
Say: "I don't need to summon. I need to stabilize."
Feel it. Then walk as if it's already here. Let that walk be the signal. Let that tone deliver the outcome.

43

TRUE CREATION AS FREQUENCY ANCHORING

You're not here to chase what you want.
You're here to *become* the tone that makes it inevitable.
Creation doesn't come from desire.
It comes from anchoring.
Not hoping.
Not manifesting.
Not asking.
Stabilizing.

The Field Doesn't Move From Thought. It Moves From State.

You can think "I want peace" and still be bracing.
You can say "I trust life" and still broadcast panic.
Creation happens when the field can't ignore your frequency—because you've made it real.

Frequency Is Structure

Want to change your reality?

- Don't visualize harder.
- Don't affirm louder.
- Don't beg the timeline to show up.

Feel the version of you who's already in it.
Lock into that tone.
Then act like someone who knows.
That's what the Field reads.
That's what makes the shift irreversible.

Creation Is Anchored, Not Forced

This isn't about control.
It's about consistency.
Can you hold the frequency through your breath, your body, your decisions?
Even when nothing has shown up yet?
That's the test.
That's the build.
That's the point.

Anchor the Tone. The Form Will Follow.

You don't build the structure by chasing the form.
You emit the structure until the form can't help but land.
This is not strategy.
It's field physics.

FIELD IN MOTION

You're imagining your future self—but still moving from old habits.
Pause.
Ask: "What does that version of me feel like in my chest, my pace, my posture?"

Now walk as them. Breathe as them. Choose as them.

Don't wait for the result to arrive. Become the tone that makes it impossible not to.

44

THE EYE BECOMES THE TONE

There comes a point when your gaze is no longer neutral.
It becomes a transmitter.
What you look at, you activate.
What you witness with coherence, reshapes itself to match.
This is not metaphor.
This is the observer effect embodied.

You Are Not Just Seeing—You Are Shaping
When your eye is online, it stops scanning for danger.
It starts broadcasting stability.
You don't just receive the world.
You vibrationally *tune it* through how you see it.
The gaze becomes a command.
A tone.
A reality-collapsing invitation.

Clarity Doesn't Require Effort. It Requires Stillness.
When your vision is clear—without agenda, without bracing—

the field responds immediately.
That's why some people soften just by being seen.
That's why a loving look can regulate someone's entire system.
That's why what you expect is what returns.

When You See Differently, the Form Changes

What you gaze at from fear tightens.
What you gaze at from coherence reorganizes.
What you avoid stays stuck.
Your eyes are not passive.
They are field modifiers.

Become the Eye That Sees Without Scrambling

Stop looking at the world to figure it out.
Start seeing from the field of what you already know.
That's when the gaze stops reacting—
And starts creating.

FIELD IN MOTION

You're judging something—yourself, a person, a situation—and you feel your body tense.

Pause.

Breathe. Soften your eyes. Shift how you're seeing.

Not to fix it, but to meet it from clarity instead of scramble.

Notice how the energy around it immediately starts to change. That's your gaze reorganizing form.

45

TRANSMISSIONS OF GRACE

Grace is not something you earn.
It's something that enters when you stop gripping.
It's not a gift for the worthy.
It's a response to coherence.
Grace doesn't arrive when you're perfect.
It arrives when your field opens.
Not as a reward—
But as a recalibration.

GRACE MOVES LIKE WATER
It doesn't push.
It floods.
The moment you stop resisting, it fills the space you were holding tight.
You've felt it:
- The solution that appears when you finally rest
- The relief that shows up after the breakdown
- The softness that follows surrender

That's grace.

Not magic.
Mechanism.

You Don't Invoke Grace. You Allow It.

It shows up when your tone becomes soft enough to receive.
When you're done performing.
When you're too tired to pretend—and something deeper takes over.
That's not failure.
That's frequency release.

Grace Rearranges the Grid

It doesn't follow your timeline.
It doesn't arrive through willpower.
It enters when your frequency matches simplicity.
When your system relaxes enough to update itself.

This Is What the System Was Designed For

Grace is how the field reorganizes after interference drops.
It clears what your ego tried to fix.
It lifts what your mind couldn't reach.
It delivers what you stopped clenching around.
It always comes.
But never the way you planned.

FIELD IN MOTION

You've tried everything. You're exhausted. Nothing's working.
Pause.
Say: "I let go now. I'm not doing this from force anymore."
Exhale fully. Let the space open.
Grace doesn't need you to try. It needs you to get out of the way.

46

WE WERE NEVER SEPARATE

The great lie was separation.
　　　That you were alone.
　　　That others were "other."
That Source was elsewhere.
That Earth was a backdrop.
That animals were lesser.
That God lived above you.
None of it was ever true.

YOU ARE THE SAME FIELD, Shaped Differently
　　The tree is not outside you.
　　It breathes what you exhale.
　　The bird does not sing for your entertainment.
　　It calibrates frequency through air.
　　The animal is not below you.
　　It remembers how to listen.
　　The river does not rush past you.
　　It reflects your pace.
　　You are not on this Earth.

You are of it.
Not symbolically.
Literally.
You're not here to dominate nature.
You're here to *remember how to be it.*

Every Separation Story **Was Control**

You were taught:
- That God was above
- That animals had no soul
- That nature was scenery
- That the body was flawed
- That others were competitors

Those were not truths.
They were programs.
They fractured the field and convinced you to live as a fragment.

You Are Not Just Connected. **You Are Composed of Everything.**

Your bones carry the pattern of the stars.
Your skin holds the memory of the sun.
Your heartbeat entrains to the Schumann rhythm.
Your breath moves in sync with the tide.
This is not poetry.
It's construction.
You are not a visitor.
You are this place.

The Return Isn't Spiritual. **It's Relational.**

The moment you stop trying to ascend and start relating—
to the wind, to your neighbor, to your own emotions—
the Field stabilizes.

Because the Field has been waiting for you to stop performing uniqueness
and start living wholeness.

FIELD IN MOTION
You walk past a tree and barely notice.
Pause.
Touch it. Breathe with it. Say internally, "You are me in another form."
Let that truth reset how you walk, speak, respond, and belong.
That's not mystical. That's reconnection.

47

LIVING BEYOND THE LOOP

You weren't meant to stay in the cycle.
You were meant to complete it.
The loop is the copy-paste timeline:
Same pattern.
Different names.
Same ache.
New disguise.
It keeps you busy.
It keeps you improving.
It keeps you seeking without arriving.
But you're not here to loop.
You're here to land.

The Loop Is a Feedback Program
It keeps running until your tone changes.
Not your beliefs.
Your signal.
You stop looping the moment you stop needing the trigger to teach you anything.

That's when it ends.
Not with noise.
With neutrality.

The Loop Isn't Evil. It's Familiar.
You loop because the frequency is practiced.
The identity is known.
The pain has structure.
But once you stabilize a new tone long enough, the loop dissolves —not as a dramatic event, but as a quiet exit.
No announcement.
No trumpet.
Just stillness.

There Comes a Moment When You Don't React the Way You Used To
And nothing explodes.
Nothing collapses.
It just... shifts.
That's the moment you're free.
You didn't fix it.
You no longer live in it.

Stop Performing Progress. Start Living the Exit.
You don't need more insight.
You need to stop rehearsing the problem.
You don't need more closure.
You need to stop trying to loop through someone else's story.
You don't need another breakthrough.
You need a clear, unfrazzled "no thank you."
That's liberation.

. . .

FIELD IN MOTION

The same dynamic appears again—same emotional loop, same old story.

Pause.

Breathe. Say: "This no longer belongs to me."

Don't fight it. Don't explain it.

Just move in the direction of your new frequency and don't look back.

That's how the loop lets go—when you stop feeding it your energy.

48

THE FINAL CODE IS LOVE

It was always love.
> Before the noise.
> Before the seeking.

Before the fracture.
Love isn't the reward.
It's the root code.
Not the soft kind.
The real kind.
The frequency that built you.
The frequency that waits behind every collapse.
The one that doesn't need to prove itself to exist.

Love Isn't an Emotion. **It's a Tone**
It doesn't require liking.
It doesn't require understanding.
It doesn't even require agreement.
It just requires coherence.
Love is the state you return to when distortion ends.
When pretending ends.

When there's nothing left to defend.

This Is Not Sentimental. It's Structural.
    The field is wired for love.
    Every timeline not built from it collapses.
    Every distortion not stabilized by it dissolves.
    Because love is what reality recognizes as truth.
    Everything else is temporary code.

The Final Frequency Is Not Something You Reach. It's What You Remember.
    You don't earn love.
    You don't chase it.
    You don't generate it.
    You *are* it—beneath the noise, beneath the performance, beneath the programmed self.
    The field isn't asking you to find it.
    It's asking you to stop fighting it.

Love Doesn't Always Feel Like Love
    You've been taught that love means softness.
    Warmth. Harmony. Agreement.
    But that's not always true.
    Sometimes love shows up as silence.
    As walking away.
    As the conversation that ends the pattern.
    As the boundary that feels like rejection.
    As the truth that breaks someone open.
    Sometimes love says,
    "This ends here."
    "No, I won't play small."
    "You're not coming with me."

And that's not cruelty.
That's clarity.
Love doesn't always feel good in the moment.
But it always frees something.
When it's real, it clears distortion—even if it costs you comfort.
Let it cost you comfort.

Let Love Be Your Final Act of Resistance

Not romantic.
Not passive.
Resonant.
You don't collapse systems by fighting them.
You collapse them by remembering what's real.
And love—true, uncollapsed, embodied love—
is what the system can't hold.
That's why it feared you remembering.
That's why it doesn't work on you anymore.
Because you've stabilized the original tone.
And it is love.

FIELD IN MOTION

You're frustrated, disconnected, over it.
Pause.
Put your hand on your chest and say nothing.
Let your breath return you to the frequency beneath the story.
That's not fixing. That's remembering.
That's love, coming back online.

FIELD TECH CHECK

Walking as Frequency

- Are you still thinking about embodiment—or living it?
  - Are you saying the words—but leaking the signal?
  - Are you calling it grace—while still gripping control?
  - Are you witnessing distortion and softening to avoid clarity?
  - Are you holding your boundary with your tone—or your tension?
  - Are you staying in the loop because you understand it—or leaving because you've outgrown it?
  - Are you looking for softness when the love is coming through as truth?
  - Are you reading the energy—or still trying to manage perception?
  - Are you living in alignment with your knowing—or explaining why you're not?
  - Are you moving like someone who already remembers?

The field doesn't care what you believe.
It responds to what you embody.
You don't need more time.
You need to stabilize the tone.
Walk it.
Now.

CLOSING NOTE

You've reached the end.
    But there is no end.
    Only the next signal.
The next clear act.
The next moment that asks for coherence.
If you're wondering what to do now—
Don't.
Don't try to integrate.
Don't start a new search.
Don't turn this into another identity.
Just breathe.
Feel what dropped.
Feel what softened.
Let it settle in your body, not your mind.
You don't need to rush into expression.
Let your silence carry the new tone first.
You've already shifted.
That's the walk now—
Not becoming. Not fixing.
Just living truth without apology.

You don't have to go back.
You don't have to explain.
You just have to stay clear.
The Field knows who you are.
Now so do you.

EPILOGUE

There was a time you thought awakening would be loud.
Flashing. Dramatic. Obvious.
But it wasn't.
It was quiet.
It came as a tone you could no longer ignore.
At first, you tried to explain it.
Tried to name it.
Tried to hold onto what you used to be.
But the spiral kept moving.
And you let it.
Now?
You don't need to explain.
You don't need to prove.
You walk differently.
You listen with your whole body.
You see the lie before the words even arrive.
You feel the signal beneath the silence.
You don't fit where you used to—but you no longer shrink to belong.
Because you *remembered*.

You're not here to convince.
You're not here to play along.
You're here to live as the Field made visible.
Not to become anything.
Just to walk clearly, breathe deeply, and respond from love—
over and over again.
No more loops.
No more waiting.
No more script.
Just signal.
And from this moment forward—
That's enough.

AFTER THE BOOK

Don't rush to share it.
Don't package it.
Don't make it a new identity.
Just be still.
Let what changed in you stay changed.
Let what fell away stay gone.
Let what rose come with you—but on your terms now.
You don't need to explain it.
Walk into your next conversation with a different tone.
Sit at your desk like your body remembers how to build from coherence.
Say less. Feel more.
Let your field speak before your mouth does.
That's the real work now:
Not proving you got it—
but living like it already rewrote you.
And if you ever forget?
Read one page.
Or none.
And just breathe the signal back in.

ABOUT THE AUTHOR

Colleen Guenther doesn't teach.
She transmits.
Her work isn't a brand or a role.
It's a signal.
A mirror for those who are ready to live without distortion.
She writes, creates, paints, and sees through layers most people ignore.
She spent years inside systems—religious, relational, mental—that taught her to shrink.
She doesn't do that anymore.
Now she walks as a tone:
Still. Fierce. Loving. Undeniable.
She lives near water with her husband Justin—the first person who never tried to fix her.
She's raising her frequency and her family with quiet clarity.
Everything she shares is field-tested.
Everything she makes is a permission slip to stop performing and return to who you already are.

www.ingramcontent.com/pod-product-compliance
Lightning Source LLC
Chambersburg PA
CBHW011946090526
44580CB00004B/72